First Lessons in Reading

S0-AQC-879

written by Eunice M. Magos
and Esther H. Hornnes
illustrated by Priscilla Burris

EUNICE M. MAGOS received a Bachelor of Science degree from New York University, and a Master's degree in Individualized Education from the College of St. Scholastica in Minnesota. She has been a director of Head Start, taught gifted primary classes and participated in the Learning to Read Through the Arts program. She has taught remedial reading and kindergarten and currently teaches first grade in the Hopatcong Borough School District in New Jersey.

ESTHER H. HORNNES received a Bachelor of Arts degree from Shelton College and William Paterson College in New Jersey. She has done graduate work at North Dakota State University and Oslo University in Oslo, Norway. She has taught grades 1-4 and presently teaches pre-school in the Hillside Nursery School in Succasunna, New Jersey.

PRISCILLA BURRIS received an Associate of Arts Degree in Creative Design from the Fashion Institute of Design and Merchandising in Los Angeles. As a free lance artist of child-related artwork, she has been drawing since she was one year old. Priscilla lives in southern California.

Copyright 1987 by **THE MONKEY SISTERS, INC.**
22971 Via Cruz
Laguna Niguel, CA 92677

ISBN 0-933606-47-8

FIRST LESSONS IN READING

These introductory lessons in reading contain activities in visual discrimination, following directions, listening skills, alphabet recognition and beginning reading using sight words.

For the visual discrimination and following directions activities, directions should be read orally giving the child time to complete the task before reading the next direction. For the other activities, give children directions and have them complete the page independently.

CONTENTS

Skill: Visual discrimination; matching

Name _____

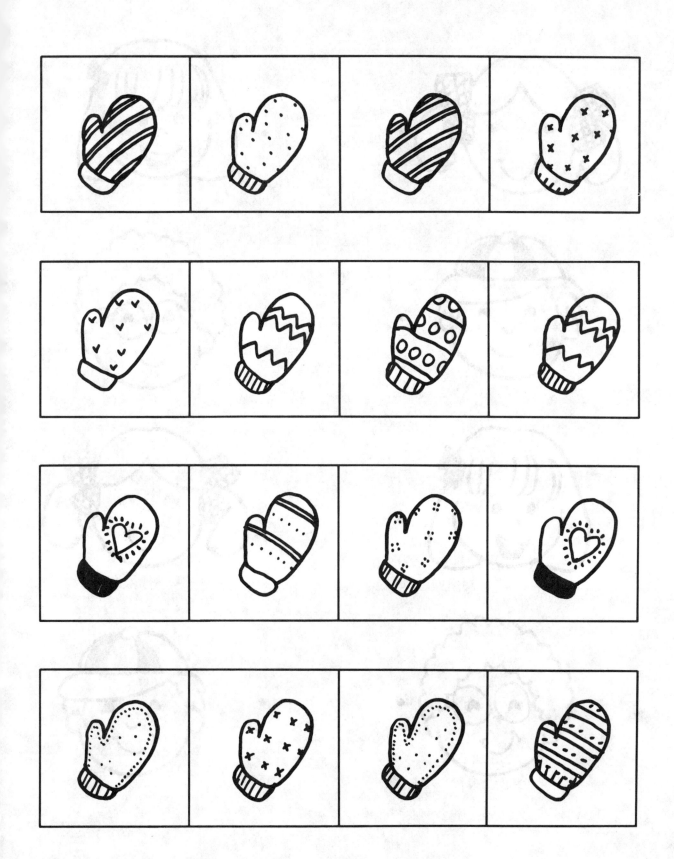

Directions: Children color the matching pair of mittens in each row.

Name _____

Directions: Children draw lines to match faces.

Name _____

Directions: Children look at the picture on the left and decide what is missing. Find the missing part on the right and circle it with a red crayon.

Name _____

Directions: Children color the ones that are the same in each row.

First Lessons in Reading © THE MONKEY SISTERS, INC.

Skill: Visual discrimination, noticing differences.

Name _____

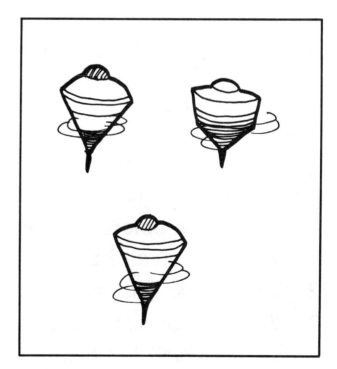

Directions: Children put an X on the object that is different in each box.

Name _____

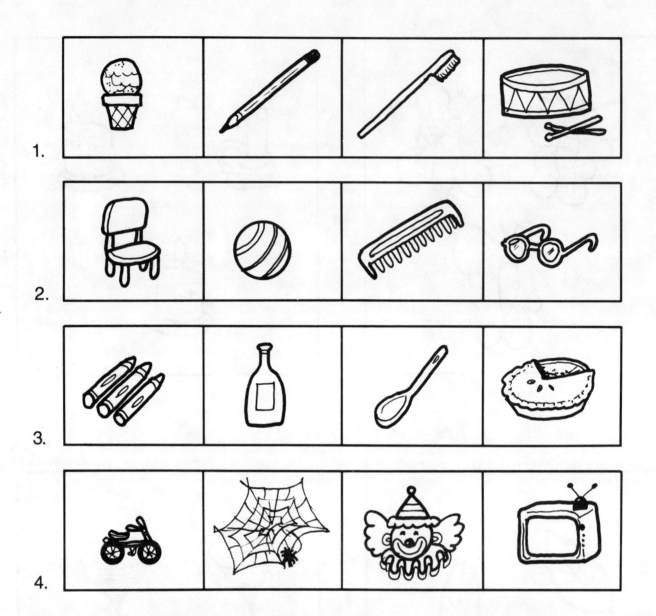

Read each direction orally. Allow time for children to complete task before reading next direction.

1. What can you eat? Color it yellow.

2. What can you play with? Draw a red line under it.

3. What can you write with? Put a blue circle around it.

4. What is funny? Put a purple X on it.

 First Lessons in Reading © THE MONKEY SISTERS, INC.

Name _____

Read each direction orally. Allow time for children to complete task before going on to next direction.

1. Put red circles around the tools.

2. Put green X's on things that are up in the air.

3. Color things that grow yellow.

4. Put brown X's on the furniture.

Name _____

1.

2.

3.

Read each direction orally. Allow time for children to complete task before reading next direction.

1. Make a red X on what you wear in the cold.
2. Color 2 things that are not round.
3. Find two things you can eat. Circle them with a brown crayon.

Name _____

Read each direction orally. Allow time for children to complete task before reading next direction.

1. Color the cup and saucer yellow.

2. Put a red X on the thing that cuts.

3. Color the fruit bowl green.

4. Draw a line around the pot on the stove.

Name _____

Time for Bed

Read each direction orally. Allow time for children to complete task before going on to next direction.

1. Dad is reading a bedtime story to the twins.
   Color their pajamas blue.
2. Draw a red line under the book.
3. Draw a green circle around the rug.
4. Put an orange box around the toy that flies.
5. Put brown X's on toys that are on the floor.

First Lessons in Reading © THE MONKEY SISTERS, INC.

Name _____

We Go Shopping

Read each direction orally. Allow time for children to complete task before reading next direction.

1. Color 4 apples red.
2. Color 3 bananas yellow.
3. Color all the grapes green.
4. Color Dad's jeans blue.
5. Color the fruitman's apron brown.

Name _____

In the Kitchen

Read each direction orally. Allow time for children to complete task before reading next direction.

1. Put three more cookies on the tray.
2. Color Mom's apron red.
3. Color two flower pots orange and one yellow.
4. Draw a blue circle around the clock.
5. Put a black circle around the mixing bowl.
6. Draw a line between the two girls.

 First Lessons in Reading © THE MONKEY SISTERS, INC.

Name _____

At the Farm

Read each direction orally. Allow time for children to complete task before reading next direction.

1. Color the horse's tail brown
2. Color two chickens yellow.
3. Put a red line above the small cow.
4. Put a blue line under the large cow.
5. Put an orange circle around the big pig.
6. Color the dog's bone brown.

Name _____

Making a Snowman

Read each direction orally. Allow time for children to complete task before reading next direction.

1. Draw a red hat on the snowman.
2. Put three buttons on him.
3. Color the tall boy's mittens blue.
4. Color the short girl's hat green.
5. Color the tall girl's boots black.
6. Put a red circle around the boy with the shovel.
7. Draw six snowballs next to the tall girl.

First Lessons in Reading © THE MONKEY SISTERS, INC.

Name _____

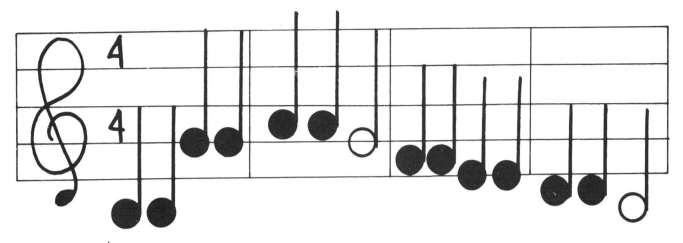

A, B, C, D, E, F, G, H, I, J, K, L, M, N,

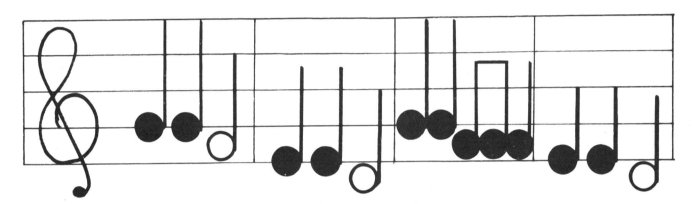

O, P, Q, R, S, T, U, V, W, X, Y, Z.

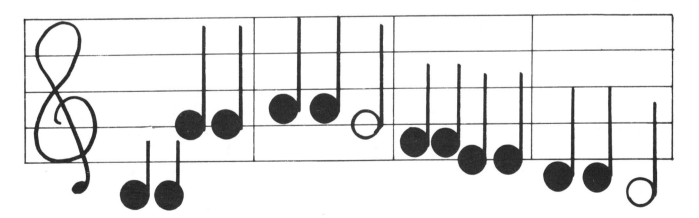

Now I sang my A B C's. Aren't you ve-ry proud of me?

Directions: Children sing alphabet song and point to letters as they sing.

Name _____

Directions: Children draw lines to match capital letters in objects. Color the pictures.

First Lessons in Reading © THE MONKEY SISTERS, INC.

Name _____

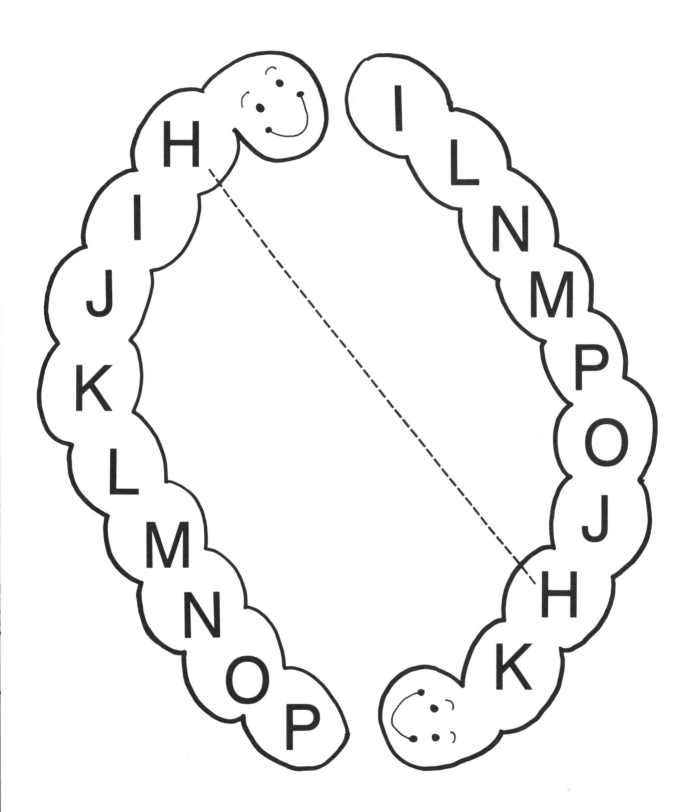

Directions: Children draw a line from the letter on the left to the one it matches on the right.

Name _____

Directions: Children cut out the letters below and glue on top of the matching letter on the wall above.

Q
R
S   T   U   V
W   X   Y   Z

First Lessons in Reading © THE MONKEY SISTERS, INC.

Name _____

1.	man	cap man man
2.	ball	ball see ball
3.	dish	dish dish run
4.	boat	boat jump boat

Read each direction orally. Allow time for children to complete task before reading next direction.

Directions:
Row 1: Put a red circle around the words that match the word on the left.
Row 2: Put a green X on the words that match the word on the left.
Row 3: Put a blue line under the words that match the word on the left.
Row 4: Put an orange box around the words that match the word on the left.

Name _____

Directions: Children color the balloons that have matching words in them.

Name _____

see •	• Run
the •	• See
run •	• Can
can •	• The

Directions: Children draw lines to match words beginning with lower-case letters to same words beginning with capital letters. Cut apart to make flash cards. Read the words.

Name _____

dog

See the [ ] run.

cat

The [ ] can run.

man

See the [ ] run.

girl

The [ ] can see.

Directions: Children read the word cards and cut them out on dotted lines. Paste them in correct boxes in sentences. Read sentences.

Name _____

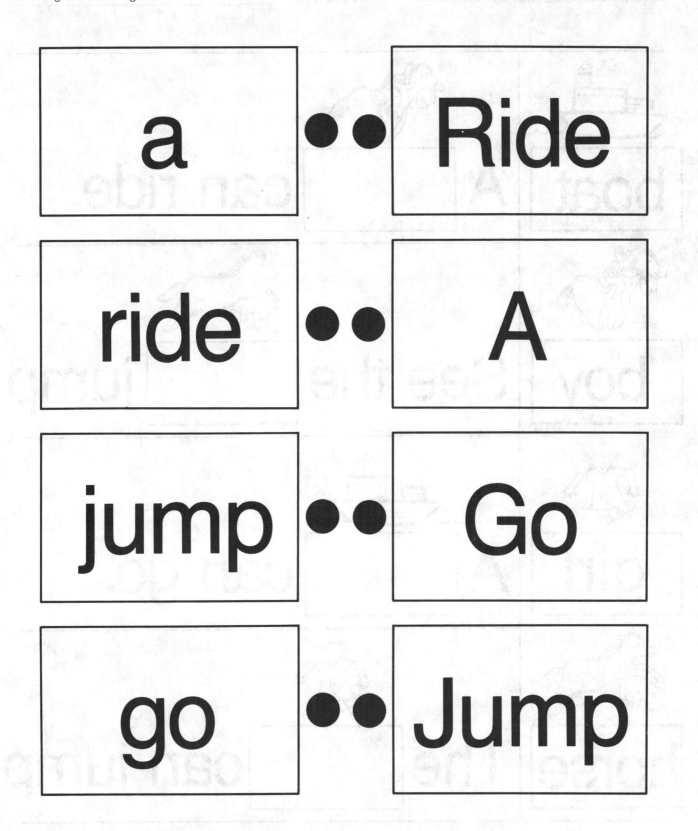

Directions: Children draw lines to match words beginning with lower case letters to same words beginning with capital letters. Cut apart to make flash cards. Read the words.

Name _____

boat

A [   ] can ride.

boy

See the [   ] jump.

girl

A [   ] can go.

horse

The [   ] can jump.

Directions: Children read the word cards and cut them out on dotted lines. Paste them in correct boxes in sentences. Read sentences.

First Lessons in Reading © THE MONKEY SISTERS, INC.

Name _____

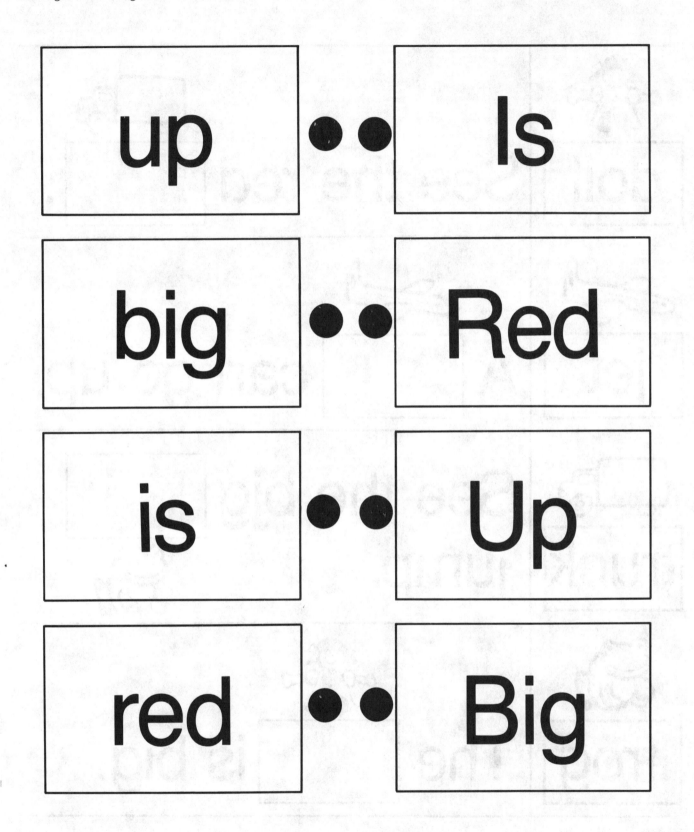

Directions: Children draw lines to match words beginning with lower case letters to same words beginning with capital letters. Cut apart to make flash cards. Read the words.

doll

See the red ____ .

jet

A ____ can go up.

truck

See the big ____ jump.

frog

The ____ is big.

Directions: Children read the word cards and cut them out on the dotted lines. Paste them in correct boxes in sentences. Read sentences.

First Lessons in Reading © THE MONKEY SISTERS, INC.

See your local school supply dealer for these products by THE MONKEY SISTERS